THE SNOW MAN

A TRUE STORY

JONAH WINTER   ILLUSTRATED BY JEANETTE WINTER

Beach Lane Books   New York   London   Toronto   Sydney   New Delhi

When he first came to the mountain,
he lived in an abandoned shack
with dirt floors,
no electricity,
no running water.

He slept in a sleeping bag.
A skunk and a pine marten lived there, too—
his only companions.
He was a young man then.

In time, he got bored.
He needed something
to fill the hours.

Outside the cabin,
all that snow
gave him an idea.

He propped up an old freezer door
to collect the snow,

then stuck a ruler in it.

Before sunrise, he got up
and measured the snow,
writing the measurements
in a little notepad.

At the end of the day,
he measured it again.

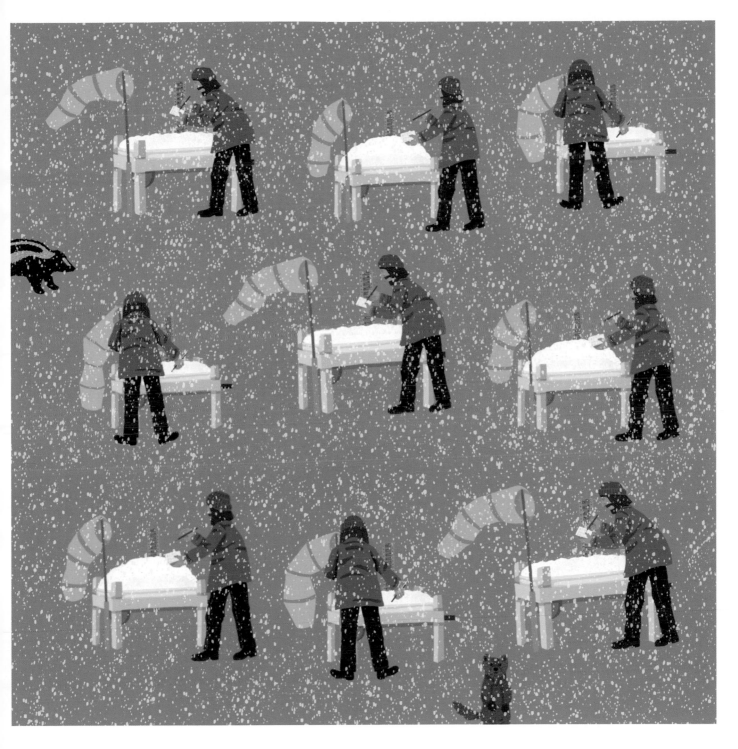

And he did this
year after year   after year after year.

He measured other things, too.
He measured the snowpack—
how much of the snow was water.

He recorded the date
of the first snowfall each winter

and the date in spring
of the first wildflower blossoms.

He noted when animals
came out of hibernation
at the end of winter.

He noted when certain birds
arrived in spring—

such as the broad-tailed hummingbirds
who always arrived just in time
to drink the nectar
of the glacier lily blossoms.

This was his life.

In time,
he built a house for himself.
It had solar panels—for electricity.

It had a freezer for storing food
and a greenhouse for growing lettuce.

It even had a movie room—
where, at night, he would sit
and watch movies from India.

He kept the house well-stocked: jars and jars
of spaghetti sauce, salad dressing, pickles,
packets of Indian food.
He froze scrambled eggs in ice trays.

He had lots of hats.

When he wasn't measuring the snow,
he was chopping wood.

Sometimes he skied into the nearest town,
eight miles away,
for supplies.

He skied 800 miles every winter.

And with every passing winter,
he grew older.
Decades passed.

He now had stacks and stacks
of notebooks filled with measurements.

In time, he noticed something interesting:
The snow was disappearing.

Year by year, the snow arrived later
and melted sooner—and there wasn't as much of it.

Animals came out of hibernation sooner.
Wildflowers bloomed sooner.

He shared his observations with a local scientist
who was studying climate change.
The scientist was amazed
by this mountain of information
collected over many years—
all inside these little notebooks.

These measurements proved that
the earth was getting warmer.
They became public information—
used by scientists all over the world.
Meanwhile, this man on the mountain
now enters his notes into a computer.

He's an old man now.
He has stopped chopping wood.
He doesn't ski as much.

For the time being, though,
he keeps on measuring the snow,

taking notes on animals and insects he sees,
wondering how long he can survive here,
alone, up on this mountain,
surrounded by trees and animals,

and, for the time being,

snow.

AUTHOR'S NOTE

The Snow Man is a true story about a real person named billy barr (he doesn't capitalize the first letters of his name), who grew up in Trenton, New Jersey, but has spent most of his life in the Rocky Mountains, living alone at the bottom of a 12,631-foot mountain in the wilderness of a ghost town called Gothic, eight miles from the nearest town with any people, Crested Butte. He first came to this location in 1972 when he was twenty-one years old, still a college student and only intending to stay for one summer. It was a summer job at the nearby Rocky Mountain Biological Laboratory—working on a water chemistry project—that drew this environmental science student to Colorado. At the end of the summer, he went back home to New Jersey, where he found himself wanting to return to this peaceful place, far from people and the commotion and complexity of the civilized world. So he dropped out of college and did return and has never left.

It wasn't an interest in the environment that first prompted him to start measuring the snow and taking notes about the wildlife in the late fall of 1973—it was, or so he says, simply boredom. There was no one to talk to (unless you count the skunk and the pine marten, who probably weren't the best conversationalists), and so he used his measurements and notes as a way of filling up the empty hours when he wasn't chopping wood or skiing to and from the nearest town.

But as the years progressed, he started noticing patterns—signs that the climate up there in the mountains was changing, getting warmer. And what started as a random pastime soon became the focus of his life—and an invaluable resource for scientists studying climate change. It was the scientists at the Rocky Mountain Biological Laboratory, where billy had done some work as an accountant over the years, who first became aware of his mountain of precious data. His notes and observations far predate any computer database of information—and as such provide incredible insight into just how long, and at what rate, the climate has been changing in alpine locales such as the Rocky Mountains. In 2016, his story made it to the news through a short film about him, *The Snow Guardian*. Since then, feature articles about him have appeared in major publications. Though he never sought fame, to say the least, he now has some.

There are lots of different ways a person can spend his life. And billy barr's way is arguably one of the more original and interesting—and useful—ones imaginable. He is now seventy-three years old.

FOR FURTHER READING AND RESEARCH

Brulliard, Karin. "He Spent Almost 50 Years Alone at 10,000 Feet. His Hobby Helped Shape Climate Research in the Rockies." *Washington Post*. November 27, 2021. https://www.washingtonpost.com/nation/2021/11/27/colorado-rockies-snow-climate-lab/.

Heim, Morgan, dir. *The End of Snow*. 2016. Day's Edge Productions. http://www.endofsnow.com/.

Johnson, Alissa. "Short Climate Film Features Gothic Local Billy Barr." *Crested Butte News*. December 22, 2016. https://crestedbuttenews.com/2016/12/short-climate-film-features-gothic-local-billy-barr/.

Phippen, J. Weston. "The Hermit Who Inadvertently Shaped Climate-Change Science." *Atlantic*. January 12, 2017. https://www.theatlantic.com/science/archive/2017/01/billy-barr-climate-change/512198/.

For Allyn
—Jonah Winter

For Dave Johnston, for his part in this
—Jeanette Winter

BEACH LANE BOOKS
An imprint of Simon & Schuster Children's Publishing Division
1230 Avenue of the Americas, New York, New York 10020
Text © 2023 by Jonah Winter
Illustration © 2023 by Jeanette Winter
Book design by Irene Metaxatos © 2023 by Simon & Schuster, Inc.
All rights reserved, including the right of reproduction in whole or in part in any form.
BEACH LANE BOOKS and colophon are trademarks of Simon & Schuster, Inc.
For information about special discounts for bulk purchases, please contact Simon & Schuster
Special Sales at 1-866-506-1949 or business@simonandschuster.com.
The Simon & Schuster Speakers Bureau can bring authors to your live event. For more
information or to book an event, contact the Simon & Schuster Speakers Bureau at
1-866-248-3049 or visit our website at www.simonspeakers.com.
The text for this book was set in Cotford Text.
Manufactured in China
0523 SCP
First Edition
2 4 6 8 10 9 7 5 3 1
CIP data for this book is available from the Library of Congress.
ISBN 9781665932394
ISBN 9781665932400 (ebook)